Follow

Follow

ANDY STANLEY

ZONDERVAN

Follow Participant's Guide
Copyright © 2014 by North Point Ministries, Inc.

This title is also available as a Zondervan ebook. Visit www.zondervan.com/ebooks.

Requests for information should be addressed to:

Zondervan, 3900 *Sparks Dr. SE, Grand Rapids, MI 49546*

ISBN 978-0-310-82354-4

Cover design: Studio Gearbox
Cover photography: iofoto / Shutterstock
Interior design: Mike Davis

First Printing June 2014 / Printed in the United States of America

Contents

Introduction

THE GAME
By Andy Stanley

I grew up in the church. I'm a pastor's kid, so the whole church thing was just part of my daily life. Pastors' kids see church differently than everyone else. We see it less mystically. I remember hearing people say, "I just felt the Spirit of God in the room," and thinking, *No, the room was full; that's all.* Whenever the room is full, people feel the Spirit of God. Take that same group of a thousand or so people and assemble them in a 50,000-seat football stadium and they won't feel the Spirit. That was my view growing up as a pastor's kid, anyway. I don't know where I got that idea, but it was wrong ... and really cynical.

Around the time I entered high school, I started feeling like the Christian life—in fact, all religion and spirituality—was just a giant game of "Jesus Says." You know how to play Simon Says, right? If Simon says it, you do it. If Simon doesn't say it, you don't do it. When I was a kid, that's how being a Christian felt. Jesus says pray. Jesus says go to church. Jesus says don't say that word. Jesus says don't look over there.

If I did what Jesus said, I was okay. If I didn't, I was out of the game. The problem was that the game was so demanding and dull, it was almost a relief to be out. Who wants to live life as though it's a random series of *dos* and *don'ts* created by a God who seems to just want to make things difficult?

My faith might have shriveled up and disappeared, except that every summer I'd go to camp and decide I needed to get back into the Jesus Says game. I needed to take things more seriously. I needed to commit to praying, reading my Bible, and doing everything else Jesus called me to do. I needed to try harder.

But I was miserable. In fact, here's something else I noticed about playing Jesus Says. Even when I was successful, when I was doing everything (or almost everything) I thought Jesus was calling me to do, I would look around at the people who weren't and judge them. They should be playing harder. If they took the game more seriously, they might be winning ... like me. After all, if I was going to be miserable playing this awful game of Jesus Says, I wanted them to be miserable too. The better I played Jesus Says, the more judgmental I got. The more judgmental I got, the meaner I got. How messed up is that? The truth is, I was kind of jealous of people who weren't playing Jesus Says because they seemed to be having more fun than I was having.

Maybe you gave up on church at one time in your life. Maybe

you thought about giving up on church. Maybe you did so or thought about doing so because you grew up in a church or a religious system that was all about playing Jesus Says. And you just weren't good at it. You weren't consistent. You didn't have the discipline to be whatever it was religion said you should be. So you quit. Or you cling desperately to your faith but find no joy in it.

Here's some great news. If you could somehow erase everything you've heard about God, Jesus, the Bible, and religion, and start with a blank slate, you'd find that the writers of the Gospels—Matthew, Mark, Luke, and John—didn't present faith as a game of Jesus Says. In fact, they said faith is extraordinarily relational. They claimed Jesus didn't come so we can do whatever arbitrary thing he says, but so we can learn to live like children of God ... to *follow him.*

So, that's what this study is all about. Regardless of where you are on the spectrum of faith, Jesus' invitation to follow is for you.

Session 1

JESUS SAYS

Jesus extended an invitation to follow to every single kind of person imaginable—rich people, poor people, people who were spiritual, people who weren't spiritual. He didn't place a bunch of conditions on his offer. He just invited them to follow.

One account of Jesus inviting someone to follow him is found in the gospel written by Matthew. Matthew was one of Jesus' followers. In this part of his gospel, he tells a story about himself. The story introduces us to the profound but simple idea of following Jesus. Here is what Matthew wrote:

> As Jesus went on from there, he saw a man named Matthew sitting at the tax collector's booth. "Follow me," he told him, and Matthew got up and followed him.
> **Matthew 9:9**

Simple, right? But in Jesus' culture, tax collectors were the lowest of the low. They were Jewish people collecting Roman taxes from other Jews. They were hated. They were outcasts. They couldn't go to the temple. They couldn't be a part of society. They could only hang out with other tax collectors because even sinners didn't want to be around them.

Jesus could have walked up to Matthew and said sarcastically, "I bet your mother is really proud you!" Jesus was considered a rabbi. All of the harsh and disapproving things he could have or should have said to Matthew would have been justified as far as the culture around them was concerned. But Jesus looked at Matthew the tax collector and said, "Follow me."

The crowd surrounding Jesus and Matthew probably thought they'd misheard Jesus. They must have been confused. Surely he didn't say, "Follow me." But that's exactly what Jesus said. And Matthew would never forget it. Those two words, spoken by Jesus, changed his life forever.

How radical was Jesus' call to Matthew? When all eyes were on the Son of God, he chose to reach out to a tax collector. Was he approving of Matthew's life? Was he saying, even indirectly, that sin didn't matter?

DISCUSSION STARTER

Talk about one of your favorite bosses, coaches, or teachers. What made it easy for you to follow that person?

VIDEO OVERVIEW
For Session 1 of the DVD

Jesus was extraordinarily comfortable with people who weren't anything like him. Based on what we read in Matthew, Mark, Luke, and John, people who were nothing like Jesus were extraordinarily comfortable with him too. Have you ever met someone who is so comfortable with himself, he makes everyone else comfortable? Jesus was like that ... a hundredfold. That's a big deal because Jesus was God in a body. He wasn't obligated to make everyone around him feel comfortable. Based on all the sin in the world, he would have been entirely justified in making everyone feel *uncomfortable*.

But Jesus was so comfortable in his own skin that he didn't hesitate to hang out with sinners, outcasts, lowlifes, and even tax collectors like Matthew. Most of us avoid people like that because we worry about what other people—"better" people—will think if they see us. If I hang around with the broken and dysfunctional, people will assume I'm broken and dysfunctional, too, right?

In fact, that's exactly what the Pharisees—the religious leaders of Jesus' day—wondered about Jesus. The Bible records their response:

When the Pharisees saw this, they asked his disciples, "Why does your teacher eat with tax collectors and sinners?"
Matthew 1:11

It's easy to dismiss the Pharisees as being small-minded and intolerant, but put in the same situation, we'd all be tempted to ask the same question. After all, Jesus was like them. He was a rabbi and they were rabbis. He was a law-keeper and they were law-keepers. He was holy and they were holy. So, why would Jesus choose to hang out with people who were nothing like him—people who were far from God—instead of hanging out with people who believed in the same religious rules and traditions?

Here's how Jesus answered their question:

On hearing this, Jesus said, "It is not the healthy who need a doctor, but the sick."
Matthew 9:12

Now, imagine that Matthew was sitting right there when Jesus responded to the Pharisees. He heard what Jesus said. A guest in his home, at his dinner table, called him and his friends "the sick." Maybe Matthew was offended. Or maybe, because he was a tax collector, he already knew he was sick.

The truth is, when it comes to sin, we're all sick. We're not even consistent at keeping the rules we set for ourselves, let alone keeping God's rules. If you're a parent, you probably set rules for your kids that you don't even keep. All parents do that. No one is perfect. Deep down, we all know that if our relationship with God depends on how we keep his rules, we're in trouble.

Jesus changed all that. He shared meals with sinners. He didn't pretend they were okay. He made it clear that he knew *they* were sinners and he knew they knew they were sinners. But he was so comfortable in his own skin that he didn't worry about what the Pharisees or anyone else thought about the company he chose to keep. This is what he told the Pharisees next:

> *"But go and learn what this means: 'I desire mercy, not sacrifice.' For I have not come to call the righteous, but sinners."*
> **Matthew 9:13**

Jesus didn't worry that others would think less of him. Instead, he invited those who were far from God to experience God's love … by following him. He wasn't content to just be with people who believed all the right things or behaved in all the right ways. He wanted to join with the people who believed all the right things and behaved in all the right ways in order to call those who didn't.

This is important because it means the church all over the world can't become a place that is content to gather together and believe the right things and behave in the right ways and stop there. If we do, we'll find ourselves outside the room Jesus inhabits when he comes to call the sick and the sinners who need a Savior.

It's not enough to believe right. It's not enough to behave right. Christians who are content with that eventually become Pharisees. They become judgmental. They become the ones who demand that others change before they can begin to follow Jesus.

But Jesus called sinners and unbelievers to follow him. He didn't demand that they change first. He didn't even demand that they believe he was the Son of God. He knew that if they just followed, if they just took a step in his direction, it would change them.

VIDEO NOTES

If you are willing to _____ follow me.
Am I following?

Matthew's only friends were other tax collectors + sinners. (Many were at Matthews house with Jesus + His disciples.

DISCUSSION QUESTIONS

1. Did you grow up in a church that emphasized doing what Jesus says over following him? Or if you didn't grow up going to church, did you assume that's what Christianity was all about? How has the "Jesus says" mindset affected your spiritual journey so far?

2. Jesus was extraordinarily comfortable with people who were nothing like him. How might your community, your nation, and the world be different if the church treated people the way Jesus did?

3. In Jesus' culture, tax collectors were considered the lowest of the low. What kinds of people occupy that position in our culture? Is it challenging for you to believe that Jesus would extend an offer to those people to follow him? Why or why not?

4. How comforting is the idea that Jesus wants everyone to follow him regardless of what they believe or how they behave? How is it challenging?

5. What are some things that make it difficult for you to follow Jesus?

6. What is one thing you can do this week to begin to follow Jesus or to follow him more closely? What can this group do to support you?

MOVING FORWARD

Jesus' invitation to follow is for you.

Being a sinner doesn't disqualify you; it's a prerequisite. Being an unbeliever doesn't disqualify you. The invitation to follow is purely an invitation to relationship. It's not an invitation to obedience. It's an invitation to a relationship with your Father in heaven.

CHANGING YOUR MIND

Then he called the crowd to him along with his disciples and said: "Whoever wants to be my disciple must deny themselves and take up their cross and follow me."

Mark 8:34

PREPARATION FOR SESSION 2

To prepare for Session 2, use these devotions during the week leading up to your small group meeting.

DAY ONE

Read Romans 2:1-2. Consider our tendency to judge one another. What does faith look like when we let God judge others instead of doing so ourselves? *You, therefore, have no excuse you who pass judgment on someone else, for at whatever point you judge others, you are condemning yourself, because you who pass judgment do the same thing (2) Now we know that God's judgment against those who do such things is based on truth (His judgment is right)*

DAY TWO

Read Romans 2:1-4. Have you ever considered our tendency to judge others as contempt for God's kindness, forbearance, and patience? In what ways has God's kindness led you to repentance? *(3) And since you do the same things as those people you judge, surely you understand that God will judge you too. How do you think you will be able to escape His judgment? (4) God has been kind to you. He has been very patient, waiting for you to change. But you think no thing of His kindness. Maybe you don't understand that God has been kind to you so that you DAY THREE will decide to change your lives.*

DAY THREE

Read Luke 5:1-5. Have you ever felt God's call for you to do something that didn't make sense? If so, what happened? How did that experience change your faith? *Ministry of prison ministry, It has given me a new insight on people & the consequences of their actions on their lives. How God can make a difference & can give them a new beginning even where they are.*

DAY FOUR

Read Luke 5:1–8. Like Simon Peter in verse 8, no one's faith can match God's abundance. When have you experienced this principle?

DAY FIVE

Read Luke 5:1–11. Letting down their nets was a single step that led to a lifetime of growing faith for Simon Peter, James, and John. What was your first step of faith?

When I first became a Christian at age 9.

Session 2

NEXT STEPS

Last session, we made a few big discoveries related to following Jesus. The first is that being a sinner doesn't disqualify you from following Jesus. In fact, the only people Jesus invited to follow him were sinners. The Bible records the odd fact that the people who believed the right things and behaved in the right way were the least able to understand Jesus because they were the most likely to be offended by the fact he kept inviting the most unlikely characters to follow him.

Our second big discovery was that being a nonbeliever doesn't disqualify you from following Jesus. Nobody who followed Jesus in the first century initially believed he was the Son of God. They didn't know who he was. By our definitions, they just thought he was a great teacher. Jesus didn't demand that they believe he was the Son of God before they began following him. He just called them to follow.

Here's another important thing to know about Jesus' invitation to follow him. It's not a religious invitation at all. The religion of Jesus' day—in fact, the religion of *every generation*—requires people to change before they can join. That drives nonbelievers away from the church. Sometimes, it drives believers out of the church, because they begin to believe they aren't good enough. They begin to believe they aren't religious enough. They begin to believe they aren't "church people."

Jesus came along and did some things that were disturbing to religious people: He said: join first and then you'll change. He told people to get close to him, follow him, listen, take a few notes, and over time they would change. The change might happen slowly, steadily, and imperceptibly, but it *would* happen. That's because change is a process. It's a result of a relationship with the Savior. We change when we experience the kindness of God because, as the apostle Paul wrote in Romans 2:4, it's his kindness that leads us to repentance.

So, as we begin to follow Jesus, what does it look like to take a next step?

DISCUSSION STARTER

Talk about a major goal you've achieved in your life. When you first set that goal for yourself, did it feel unachievable? How did you go about pursuing it?

VIDEO OVERVIEW
For Session 2 of the DVD

Last session, we looked at the story of how Jesus called Matthew, a tax collector, to follow him. This session, let's take a look at a passage from the gospel of Luke. It describes when Jesus called Simon, James, and John to follow him.

One day as Jesus was standing by the Lake of Gennesaret, the people were crowding around him and listening to the word of God. He saw at the water's edge two boats, left there by the fishermen, who were washing their nets. He got into one of the boats, the one belonging to Simon, and asked him to put out a little from shore. Then he sat down and taught the people from the boat.

When he had finished speaking, he said to Simon, "Put out into deep water, and let down the nets for a catch."

Simon answered, "Master, we've worked hard all night and haven't caught anything. But because you say so, I will let down the nets."

When they had done so, they caught such a large number of fish that their nets began to break. So they signaled their partners in the other boat to come and help them, and they came and filled both boats so full that they began to sink.

When Simon Peter saw this, he fell at Jesus' knees and said, "Go away from me, Lord; I am a sinful man!" For he and all his companions were astonished at the catch of fish they had taken, and so were James and John, the sons of Zebedee, Simon's partners.

Then Jesus said to Simon, "Don't be afraid; from now on you will fish for people." So they pulled their boats up on shore, left everything and followed him.
Luke 5:1–11

There are some important features to this passage that explain what it looks like to follow Jesus. Simon, James, and John experienced an event that planted a seed of faith. But it wasn't blind faith. Their decision to follow unfolded in three distinct steps:

1. They listened.

The story records that Jesus sat in Simon's fishing boat and taught a crowd of people who were gathered on the shore of the lake. Simon, James, and John heard what Jesus had to say.

2. They inconvenienced themselves.

Simon, James, and John were fishermen. Jesus was a carpenter and a rabbi. Yet when Jesus told them to go out into deep water and let down their nets, they did so even though it didn't make any sense. Letting down their nets must have seemed like a waste of time and effort, but they did it. Simon told Jesus why: "Because you say so." Their motivation was simple. It had everything to do with who Jesus was.

3. They took a single step that allowed God's faithfulness to enter their lives.

Simon, James, and John obeyed; God was faithful; and God's faithfulness encouraged them to take another step of faith ... a bigger step of faith. They "left everything and followed him."

Simon, James, and John had a little bit of information *before* they started following. But their choice to follow changed the entire trajectory of their lives. God did things in them and through them they could never have imagined that day they let down their nets. We're still reading about many of those things today.

Christianity isn't a blind faith. It's an informed faith. Following Jesus always begins with being informed. God never asks that we express blind faith. Why would he? He's God. He's capable of reaching out to us in ways that help us to take a step toward him, help us to follow.

VIDEO NOTES

Being a sinner does not dis qualify you from
following Jesus.
✓All were unbelievers in the first century
Jesus; join us and you will change,
Faith is built on information.
Faith is about information
following is about listening.
* They had another day of work ahead
of them to prepare fish for sale.
This is the beginning of the relationship
with Jesus.
They listened, inconvienienced themselves
then acted.
   Peter loaned Jesus his boat
1) sit and listen
2) be willing to ..... (leave nets)
3) change relationship - leave nets
4)

DISCUSSION QUESTIONS

1. Have you ever met a Christian whose faith impressed and intimidated you? How did that person influence your view of Christianity? How did he or she influence your view of your own faith?

2. Andy challenged you to answer the question, "Am I following Jesus?" As you thought about that question, where did it lead you?

3. What risks do you associate with following Jesus? How do those risks cause you to hesitate?

4. Do you agree with the idea that Christianity isn't a blind faith but an informed faith? Why or why not?

5. In the video, Andy talked about four stages of following Jesus—listening and learning; taking a small, inconvenient step; allowing Jesus to do something unusual in one area of your life; and surrendering all aspects of your life to him. Which stage best describes where you are right now? Explain.

6. Based on where you are right now, what is your next step in following Jesus? What can this group do to support you?

MOVING FORWARD

Your next step in following Jesus may be to continue to put yourself in environments where you can listen to what God has to say in order to make informed decisions about faith.

Maybe, like Peter in that passage from Luke's gospel, it's time to lend Jesus your boat. He's calling you to inconvenience yourself on his behalf. That inconvenience may look like opening a Bible and reading the New Testament each morning. It may look like being open and transparent with a group of believers who can encourage you to grow while holding you accountable.

Maybe you're beyond that first simple step of inconvenience. Maybe it's time for you to allow Jesus to do something unusual in one area of your life. Or maybe it's time for you to surrender all aspects of your life to him.

Whatever your next step is, if you don't take it you'll never know what God might have done in your life and through your life. So, take that next step.

CHANGING YOUR MIND

"Come, follow me," Jesus said, *"and I will send you out to fish for people."*
Matthew 4:19

PREPARATION FOR SESSION 3

To prepare for Session 3, use these devotions during the week leading up to your small group meeting.

DAY ONE

Read Luke 23:32-38. As you imagine the scene of Jesus' crucifixion, focus especially on verse 34. How does it reflect the abundance of God's kindness, forbearance, and patience mentioned last week in Romans 2:1-4?

DAY TWO

Read Luke 23:39-43. How does this challenge most people's assumptions about how a relationship with God works? How does it challenge your own assumptions?

DAY THREE

Read Matthew 10:16-18. Why do you think Jesus would send his followers out on their own? Think about a time when he asked you to do something outside of your comfort zone. How did the experience benefit you?

DAY FOUR

Read Matthew 10:19-23. When have you had to rely on the Holy Spirit during challenging circumstances?

DAY FIVE

Read Matthew 10:24-25. In what ways do these verses challenge your assumptions about the Christian life?

Session 3

FEARLESS

People assume there's a reward for following Jesus. They assume that if they choose to obey, God will pay them back in some way. They believe that when they're 70 or 80 years old, they'll be able to look back on their lives and see tangible evidence of the benefits of Jesus. They'll be glad they made the decisions they made.

Many people assume that if they follow Jesus, they'll be better people. It's true that following Jesus does make you more generous, more loving, kinder, and quicker to forgive. You'll be a better father, mother, student, husband, wife, employee, or boss. But being a better person isn't the reward for following Jesus.

Others think that if they follow Jesus, they'll go to heaven. That's true, but if you read the Gospels, you won't find Jesus calling people to follow him so they can make it to heaven. While Jesus talks a lot about the kingdom of God and the kingdom of heaven, he doesn't really attach following him with where we will spend eternity.

Check out the story of the criminal on the cross in Luke 23:32-43. After admitting that his crimes warrant the punishment of crucifixion, the criminal asks Jesus to remember him when he comes into his kingdom.

> *Jesus answered him, "Truly I tell you, today you will be with me in paradise."*
> **Luke 23:43**

Clearly, paradise isn't a reward for following Jesus. Despite his change of heart, the criminal was already nailed to a piece of wood and hours away from death. His opportunity to follow Jesus had passed.

There *is* a reward for following Jesus. It's just not what most people assume it is.

If the reward isn't being a better person and it's not heaven, what is it? What is the end game of following Jesus? What's the payoff? What's the benefit? If you decide for this next season of your life to be a follower of Jesus, what will you get out of it?

DISCUSSION STARTER

Are you superstitious in any areas of your life? Explain.

VIDEO OVERVIEW
For Session 3 of the DVD

Being a better person or going to heaven may not be the rewards for following Jesus, but there is a place God wants to take you. We get a glimpse of this destination in a passage from Matthew's gospel. In it, Jesus was about to send his disciples out on their own to proclaim the kingdom of heaven in nearby towns. Before he sent them, he delivered a pep talk that wasn't particularly peppy:

"I am sending you out like sheep among wolves. Therefore be as shrewd as snakes and as innocent as doves. Be on your guard; you will be handed over to the local councils and be flogged in the synagogues. On my account you will be brought before governors and kings as witnesses to them and to the Gentiles. But when they arrest you, do not worry about what to say or how to say it. At that time you will be given what to say, for it will not be you speaking, but the Spirit of your Father speaking through you.

"Brother will betray brother to death, and a father his child; children will rebel against their parents and have them put to death. You will be hated by everyone because of me, but the one who stands firm to the end will be saved. When you are persecuted in one place, flee to another.

Truly I tell you, you will not finish going through the towns of Israel before the Son of Man comes.

"The student is not above the teacher, nor a servant above his master. It is enough for students to be like their teachers, and servants like their masters. If the head of the house has been called Beelzebul, how much more the members of his household!
Matthew 10:16–25

That's pretty harsh. Jesus said this stuff to his inner circle of followers, the twelve men who were most committed to following him. They must have been confused as he gazed into their futures and described all of the terrible things that would happen to them. They had probably imagined that following Jesus would come with a lot of benefits. Instead, this man they'd given up everything for was describing all the ways they'd suffer as a result of their association with him.

Here's some bad news. The same message applies to us. Here's some better news. We're probably not going to face the kinds of extreme hardships the twelve disciples did. It's unlikely we'll be arrested for our faith, flogged, or persecuted so severely there's a genuine danger of death. But we will face hardship. Everyone faces hardship. It's just how life works.

But then Jesus said this:

> *"So do not be afraid of them, for there is nothing concealed that will not be disclosed, or hidden that will not be made known. What I tell you in the dark, speak in the daylight; what is whispered in your ear, proclaim from the roofs. Do not be afraid of those who kill the body but cannot kill the soul. Rather, be afraid of the One who can destroy both soul and body in hell. Are not two sparrows sold for a penny? Yet not one of them will fall to the ground outside your Father's care. And even the very hairs of your head are all numbered. So don't be afraid; you are worth more than many sparrows."*
>
> **Matthew 10:26-31**

Jesus introduced his disciples to an important idea. The good news for us is that his disciples didn't get it until the very end, until after Jesus had been crucified and God had raised him from the dead. Grasping the idea he introduced was an ongoing process for them. It's an ongoing process for us too.

He told them that even though sparrows are essentially worthless, God is aware of each and every one of them. That matters because each and every person has value to God. He numbers the hairs on each of our heads. So, if he pays attention to insignificant sparrows, we don't have to worry that he's unaware of or apathetic to the details of our lives. We don't have to be afraid.

That's huge because too often fear determines the quality and the direction of people's lives. It prevents them from taking chances. It undermines their happiness. It stops them from living up to their full potential.

But it's important to understand exactly what Jesus is offering. He didn't say, *Don't be afraid because I won't let bad things happen to you.* That's magic. Jesus wasn't a magician. He was a Savior. He said, *Don't be afraid when bad things happen because God knows you and he loves you.* That's confidence in God—a confidence so big and so sure of God's presence that it overwhelms our fear.

VIDEO NOTES

followseries.org

°Better person by following Jesus.

Pain free - problem free - not a promise.

Jesus is not magic.

Followers - people in His town, groupies, followers.

Matthew 10:29 Do not be afraid - God will take care of you. (when bad things happen)

Confidence only in God.

Mark 4:40 ←→ cuz ↗ p ∿ of X

Overwhelming faith allows us to love other people?

Perfect love

Romans 8:35

John 16:33

DISCUSSION QUESTIONS

1. Do you tend to be a worrier or do you deal with circumstances as they come? How is that natural wiring a strength for you? How is it a weakness?

2. What circumstances, consequences, or possibilities do you fear? How does that fear limit your choices in life?

3. Think about a time when you felt close to God. Were your circumstances at that time good or bad? How did those circumstances, good or bad, influence your relationship with God?

4. Have you ever met someone who was choosing to trust God through difficult circumstances? Can you imagine yourself having a faith like that? Why or why not?

5. What hopes or dreams might you miss out on if you were to let fear control your life?

6. What circumstances do you face right now that you need to entrust to God? What worries are you struggling with that you need to entrust to God? What can this group do to support you?

MOVING FORWARD

Having confidence in God honors him. But there's another reason he wants you to develop that kind of overwhelming faith. It frees you to love other people. It's the only kind of faith that will free you to love an ex-husband or ex-wife who is always on your case. It's the only kind of faith that will free you to love a boss who doesn't recognize how hard you work. It's the only kind of faith that will free you to love a wayward child who resists your wise counsel and makes a string of bad choices. It's the only kind of faith that will free you to love a parent who withholds the approval and acceptance you desire.

We all struggle to live out that kind of faith. But Jesus asks us the same question he asked his disciples again and again: *Why are you so afraid?* Maybe our confidence is still locked in our circumstances or the people who make life difficult for us. But if we focus on following Jesus, one step at a time, one day we'll get to the place where we can say, like the apostle Paul, "And we know that in all things God works for the good of those who love him, who have been called according to his purpose" (Romans 8:28).

CHANGING YOUR MIND

"I have told you these things, so that in me you may have peace. In this world you will have trouble. But take heart! I have overcome the world."

John 16:33

PREPARATION FOR SESSION 4

To prepare for Session 4, use these devotions during the week leading up to your small group meeting.

DAY ONE

Read Colossians 3:1-4. Consider what it means for your life to be "hidden with Christ in God." *When we give our lives to Christ we become new creatures in Christ. We devote our minds eyes to things of Heaven. People who do not know Christ do not see us, we are hidden in Christ.*

DAY TWO

Read Colossians 3:1-8. As you think about the two lists associated with your earthly nature (verses 5 and 8), what are some practical things you can you do to "set your heart on things above," as described in verse 1? *I think on heavenly things, not things of the world, I think about what we can do to reach others while living in this world.*

DAY THREE

Read Colossians 3:9-11. What is the relationship between "putting on the new self" (verse 10) and the recognition that in Christ there are no categories, such as Jew or Gentile, slave or free?

changing our mindset from things of this earth & what we think is important to heavenly things. We are all God's children. God doesn't categorize + we shouldn't either. Because you are Jewish or on a lower totem pole than me, or an immigrant who is only seeking a better way of life.

DAY FOUR

Read Colossians 3:12. What are some practical ways you can clothe yourself in compassion, kindness, humility, gentleness, and patience this week?

Forgiveness, Seeing others as Christ does, Keeping your mind heaven bound, not gossiping, try to understand others points of view.

DAY FIVE

Read Colossians 3:13. How does reminding yourself that God forgave you help you to be more forgiving of others? Is there anyone you need to forgive?

We are an ungrateful people. We want to be forgiven but we are not so prompted to forgive others. We want to be heaven minded but still live in the world. Remember each day things we do that displeases God and know that God has already forgiven us. Can't we be as compassionate to others if we are to mirror Christ. Once + for all give it to Christ + be done with it. Take a deep breath ____ + rest in the fact that Jesus has already forgiven them so you should to.

Session 4

FOLLOW WEAR

You can tell what a person follows by what he or she wears. Think about it. How do you recognize sports fans? They wear their team colors and logos. Dodgers fans wear blue and white. New York Knicks fans wear blue and orange. University of Georgia football fans wear red and black.

For some fans, wearing a jersey or a cap isn't enough to express the depth of their passion. They paint their faces team colors or put on outrageous costumes to let you know who they follow. Some Green Bay Packers fans wear plastic cheese wedges on their heads. The most intense Notre Dame fans dress up like leprechauns.

The things people do to express their loyalties in the world of sports may seem silly, but religious people tell you who or what they follow through the way they dress too. A Muslim woman might wear a hijab. Buddhist monks typically wear red, yellow, or orange robes. Sikh men wear dastars and grow their beards.

So, if you know who or what someone follows by what he or she wears, what should a Jesus follower wear?

If you ask nonbelievers, some would say a Jesus follower wears a gold chain with a cross on it. Others might say a Jesus follower wears a John 3:16 T-shirt. That's a nice enough sentiment but probably seems a little silly to those outside of the faith. Still others would take a darker view. They think of Christians wearing placards printed with "God Hates You" or "Sinners Burn in Hell" in bold, black letters.

But Jesus didn't call his followers to wear gold crosses, T-shirts, or placards with hateful rhetoric. When it came to follow wear, he had something entirely different and more challenging in mind.

DISCUSSION STARTER

What's your favorite sports team? To what extremes have you gone to show your support for your team?

VIDEO OVERVIEW
For Session 4 of the DVD

In Christianity, it's so easy to confuse discipline with discipleship. It's easy to assume that if we develop spiritual disciplines— reading the Bible, praying, going to church every week—it's a substitute for actually following Jesus as it relates to how we treat other people.

But spiritual discipline isn't the team colors of a Jesus follower. The apostle Paul, who spent his life planting churches all around the Mediterranean during the first century, wrote a letter to the people at the church in Colossae in Greece. In that letter, he explains what Christ followers are supposed to wear:

Colosi

> *Therefore, as God's chosen people, holy and dearly loved,*
> *clothe yourselves with compassion, kindness, humility,*
> *gentleness and patience.*
> **Colossians 3:12**

Fruit of the Spirit
Love, joy, peace, patience
Kindness, goodness, faithfulness, gentleness,
self control

Paul urges Christ followers to dress themselves up in five things:

1. Compassion

In the original Greek, the word translated here as "compassion" means to experience such overwhelming love for others that you feel it in your gut. That's a lot different than studying harder, working hard, praying harder, or going to church more often. Jesus wanted his followers first and foremost to be seen as a group of people who feel compassion for what others experience. He calls his followers to feel that compassion even when other people are wrong and have brought suffering on themselves through their poor choices.

2. Kindness

Kindness is when you loan your strength to someone else. Kindness is when people need something they can't provide for themselves, so you do it for them. You extend yourself. Kindness is unusual in this world because people rarely do something for others unless they are required to do so. Paul asserts that Jesus wants his followers to be kind to others freely, without compulsion.

3. Humility

Humility involves seeing yourself accurately in relationship with others as a result of your relationship with God. Jesus followers are nothing more than citizens of humanity, just like everyone else. Every person is loved by God. That's the great equalizer that cuts through class, wealth, education, and talent. Jesus followers approach others as peers regardless of what they do or don't do, how much they have or don't have, or how much or little they've accomplished.

4. Gentleness

For many people, gentleness has a negative connotation. We think the world punishes gentleness. You can't be gentle and get ahead. But gentleness is the decision to respond to others in light of *their* strengths and weaknesses rather than in light of our strengths. Gentle people don't enter into conversations from a position of who they are and what they've accomplished. They gear down to the level of the people with whom they are conversing. Their approach has everything to do with communication and nothing to do with condescension.

5. Patience

Patience is deciding to operate at the speed of other people. It's gearing down and saying, "You know what? I'm going to move at your speed instead of mine."

So, why does the apostle Paul urge Jesus followers to clothe themselves in compassion, kindness, humility, gentleness, and patience? What's the point? He explains in the next verse:

> *Bear with each other and forgive one another if any of you has a grievance against someone. Forgive as the Lord forgave you.*
> **Colossians 3:13**

Paul says to forgive as God has forgiven us. Be compassionate, kind, humble, and gentle to others because God has been compassionate, kind, humble, and gentle with us. How many times have we told God we'd never do something again, only to do that very thing the next month, week, or day? Yet God is patient and forgiving. And Jesus wants us to extend that same kind of patience and forgiveness to the people around us.

That's a lot different than wearing a John 3:16 T-shirt. It's definitely different than wearing a "God Hates You" placard. Paul challenges Jesus followers to wear the kind of behavior that made Jesus so attractive to people who were different from him. It's the kind of behavior that is more interested in making a difference in the lives of others than it is in making a point.

VIDEO NOTES

Apostle Paul tells Christians what
to wear in Acts. He had been a
Christian hater. Primary teachings
of Jesus John 13:34-35-36
Gravital pull is off all religions
is rule keeping & discipline.
Discipline is not discipleship.
22 years after Jesus' death, Paul
came on the scene. Colossians
3:12 Clothe yourself with compassion,
(in your bowels) kindness, (habit)
humility, (relationship with others
and with God, (love unconditionally)
gentleness, (gear down) patience
(gearing down - bear with one another,
forgive & love) and over all these
virtues; put on love.

DISCUSSION QUESTIONS

1. When you think of the word "Christian," what qualities come to mind? Are they positive or negative? Why?

2. Talk about a time when you encountered a Christian who was more interested in making a point than making a difference. How did that person affect the way you view Jesus?

3. In the video, Andy said, *"All religions gravitate toward rule keeping instead of relationship building."* Do you agree with that statement? Why or why not?

4. As you think about compassion, kindness, humility, and gentleness, which seems like it would be most difficult to live out in your relationships with others? Why?

5. Read Colossians 3:12–14. What are some of the challenges to living the kind of life Jesus calls his followers to live?

6. Think of one person in your life who is difficult to love. What is one thing you can do this week to better love that person? What can this group do to support you?

MOVING FORWARD

Jesus is less interested in spiritual disciplines, such as reading the Bible, praying, and going to church, than in our showing compassion, kindness, humility, and gentleness to the people around us. At first, that may sound too easy. But treating others as God treats us is a lot harder than reading on a regular basis, praying, or showing up at a building every week. In fact, it's so far outside our human instincts that we can't succeed without God's help.

Reach out to God and ask for his help in putting on compassion. Ask him to help you pause so you don't react to someone else based on what he or she *should* have done. Declare to God that, even though you're better than some and worse than others, all people are his children. Ask for his help in approaching others with humility. Tell your heavenly Father you want to be kind. Ask him to bring to mind opportunities to loan your strength to others. Ask him to teach you to be patient and gentle with others, to learn to move at other people's pace.

CHANGING YOUR MIND

Therefore, as God's chosen people, holy and dearly loved, clothe yourselves with compassion, kindness, humility, gentleness and patience.

Colossians 3:12

PREPARATION FOR SESSION 5

To prepare for Session 5, use these devotions during the week leading up to your small group meeting.

DAY ONE

Read Matthew 7:24–27. What challenges do you face in not just hearing Jesus' words but putting them into practice?

Fear of failure & inadequacy.

DAY TWO

Read Mark 8:31. Put yourself in the shoes of Jesus' first-century followers who didn't have full context of the crucifixion and resurrection. How do you think you would have responded to what Jesus said?

Unbelief, how could that be. However they had seen Jesus perform many miracles, even raising people from the dead.

DAY THREE

Read Mark 8:32. When has God disappointed your expectations? How did it affect your relationship with him?

DAY FOUR

Read Mark 8:33. In what ways is God currently challenging you to keep his concerns in mind rather than concerns that are "merely human"? *Peter get out of my way. You are letting Satan confuse you, Gods ways are not the same as mans.*

DAY FIVE

Read Mark 8:34. What are some practical ways a modern follower of Jesus is challenged to take up his or her cross daily? *With the business of everyday living. sometimes it is hard to take the time to listen for Gods answer to a situation. Sometimes God slows us down for that purpose. Computer games is idle business.*

Session 5

THE FINE PRINT

Contracts offer big promises. When you sign a contract for a smartphone, it details all of the stuff you'll get: access to the provider's high-speed wireless network, a certain number of minutes to talk on the phone each month, and a specified amount of data you can use to surf the Web. A contract to purchase an automobile specifies that the car belongs to you. A mortgage says that the house you're buying is your property and no one else's.

But contracts also have fine print. The fine print tells you what the benefits are going to cost you. That smartphone contract involves a monthly payment. So does buying a car or having a mortgage. Even more, the fine print tells you what will happen if you don't hold up your end of the bargain. There are financial penalties for breaking your smartphone contract before its two years are up. The car dealer can repossess your automobile if you don't make the payments. The bank can foreclose on your house.

There are a lot of benefits to following Jesus. That's pretty much what this study is about. But anyone who follows Jesus finds out in time that following costs you something. There's a price to pay. And in the moment when you're faced with the cost of following Jesus, that's when you discover who you really are. It's when you discover whether you're really a *follower* of Jesus or just a *consumer* of Jesus.

In this session we're going to take a look at what Jesus said about the cost of following him. We're going to examine the fine print.

DISCUSSION STARTER

When you were a child, what did you dream your adulthood would be like? How does your current reality align with those childhood dreams?

VIDEO OVERVIEW
For Session 5 of the DVD

If you follow Jesus, you'll be a better father, a better mother, a better spouse, a better boss, a better employee, a better person. You'll be more honest. You'll forgive more readily. You'll be more generous. You'll serve others with more enthusiasm. These are huge benefits to following Jesus.

Jesus even said that if you obey what he teaches, you'll be like a person who builds his or her house on a rock. But if you don't obey him, you'll be like a person who builds his or her house on sand. When the storms of life come, the house on the rock will stand, while the house on the sand will be washed away (Matthew 7:24-27).

You've probably seen people face extraordinary difficulty with amazing peace because they had a firm faith foundation. It probably blew your mind.

But at some point along the way, there's a price associated with following Jesus. Mark 8 tells the story of when Jesus was with his disciples in some villages around the city of Caesarea Philippi . He'd reached a critical phase of his earthly ministry. The religious authorities were getting more and more upset about his influence over people. They were beginning to plot his death.

He then began to teach them that the Son of Man must suffer many things and be rejected by the elders, the chief priests and the teachers of the law, and that he must be killed and after three days rise again. He spoke plainly about this, and Peter took him aside and began to rebuke him.

But when Jesus turned and looked at his disciples, he rebuked Peter. "Get behind me, Satan!" he said. "You do not have inmind the concerns of God, but merely human concerns."
Mark 8:31–33

Peter rebuked Jesus because he thought things were going well, and he didn't want Jesus to mess that up. Jesus was drawing large crowds. He was gaining momentum with the people. But talking about death and resurrection would only drive that crowd away. It wasn't appealing to the Jesus consumers. Jesus' response to Peter was harsh. He called him out. He told him that rather than having God's concerns in mind, Peter was focused on the personal benefits of following Jesus. He wasn't concerned about what was going to happen to Jesus. He was concerned about what was going to happen to himself because of what was going to happen to Jesus. That's not following, it's consuming.

So Jesus explained to his disciples the price they'd have to pay if they wanted to follow him ... really follow him. He gave them the fine print:

> *Then he called the crowd to him along with his disciples and said: "Whoever wants to be my disciple must deny themselves and take up their cross and follow me. For whoever wants to save their life will lose it, but whoever loses their life for me and for the gospel will save it. What good is it for someone to gain the whole world, yet forfeit their soul? Or what can anyone give in exchange for their soul?"*
> **Mark 8:34-37**

Jesus made a profound point. Imagine you have everything you could desire in this life—money, power, personal satisfaction, and the envy of other people. What if at the end of this most awesome life imaginable, you realized the cost of that life was having to forfeit eternity, forfeit your soul? Maybe that means you cease to exist. Maybe it means you're in hell. Jesus doesn't specify. But imagine you had to give up your soul for an awesome life. Would you do it? Probably not. In fact, at the end of life you'd probably trade everything you had amassed and achieved to keep your soul.

That insight is remarkable. It's life-changing.

At some point in your journey, there will be a conflict of interest. In that moment, you'll have to decide between an awesome life now and following Jesus. You'll recognize when the moment comes because it will feel like a moral imperative. It won't be something everyone else has to do. It won't be something everyone else has to stop doing. It won't be something everyone around you agrees needs to be done or not be done. Your conscience will come alive and you'll just *know* that if you're going to follow Jesus you can't go, you can't participate, you need to stay, you need to leave, you need to not call that person back, you need to not take that job. There won't be a verse or a sermon to back you up. You'll just know. And the knowing will hurt.

Following Jesus will feel a little bit like death. It may even involve the death of part of your dream. You may have waited for years for this moment to come, only to realize that you need to let it pass you by because moving forward would mean turning your back on following Jesus. But, you know what? In the long run, that moment will define who you are because you'll discover you aren't just a consumer of Jesus, you're a follower of Jesus.

It will be agonizing. It will be emotional. It will be confusing. But it will be worth it because, as Jesus promised, in giving up the life you desire you will find a better life in your Savior.

VIDEO NOTES

followseries.org
fine print
build house on rock - obeys
build house on sand - don't obey
Mark 8-27-28-33
consumer - to see what he can get
out of situation.
deny - saying no to yourself. - It costs
too much to follow Jesus.
Mark 8:35-37 If you lose your life for the
gospel will save your soul.
Salvation is free
Following Christ will eventually
cost you something.
Defining moment = you will decide
to follow Jesus.
Jer 29:11
You are going to know when that time
comes.
Do you value your soul more than
anything?

65

DISCUSSION QUESTIONS

1. Talk about a time when you knew you were supposed to do something that was difficult. Did you do it? What was the outcome?

2. Talk about a time when you've seen someone demonstrate extraordinary faith in the midst of difficult circumstances. How did that change or influence your view of faith?

Jim Elliott missionary to the Equadorian Indians, He lost his life because he refused to defend himself against those he knew God had told him to bring the faith to.

3. Have you ever seen someone else pay a price for his or her decision to follow Jesus? How did that person's experiences influence your own faith?

4. Has your faith ever cost you something? If so, how has paying that cost changed your relationship with God?

5. Read Mark 8:34–36. How do Jesus' words challenge you? In what ways do they give you comfort?

6. Are you currently being nudged to do something, say something, quit something, start something, or give up something? What can this group do to support you?

MOVING FORWARD

Each of us is writing a story with our lives. Do you want your story to be, "I couldn't say no to me" or "I decided to say no to me"? Do you want it to be "I couldn't say yes to Jesus" or "I decided to say yes to Jesus"?

Salvation is free. Being a Jesus consumer is free. Following Jesus will eventually cost you something. That's okay because what you discover about yourself and the faithfulness of your heavenly Father will be worth the cost.

CHANGING YOUR MIND

Then he called the crowd to him along with his disciples and said: "Whoever wants to be my disciple must deny themselves and take up their cross and follow me."

Mark 8:34

Romans 6:1-2

PREPARATION FOR SESSION 6

To prepare for Session 6, use these devotions during the week leading up to your small group meeting.

DAY ONE

Read Matthew 26:6–9. Consider how these verses illustrate the dangers of judging someone's behavior when we don't know what is going on in his or her heart.

DAY TWO

Read Matthew 26:10–13. The disciples made a judgment even though they didn't have all the facts. When have you been guilty of doing the same? What does that illustrate about the nature of following Jesus?

DAY THREE

Read John 12:4–6. Why do you think John includes the detail in verse 6 in his gospel? Why are his observations about Judas important to the story?

DAY FOUR

Read Matthew 16:14–16. Think about the relationship between following and Judas' betrayal. What qualities of a good follower did Judas lack?

DAY FIVE

Read Luke 5:1–5. Why would Jesus' followers demonstrate more faith in this story early in his ministry than in the story from Matthew 16, near the end of his ministry? What does this tell you about challenges you may face as you grow in faith?

Session 6

WHAT I WANT TO WANT

The primary motivation for most people to become Christians, especially when they become Christians during childhood, is to go to heaven ... or to avoid going to hell. They don't think in terms of being a Jesus follower. They don't even become Christians because they love Jesus or God. They love themselves. They want the reward of heaven, and they want to avoid the punishment of hell.

It's not that these people are shallow. That's just how the gospel is usually presented: accept Jesus into your heart so you can go to heaven. After all, who wouldn't want to go to heaven after he or she dies?

But that's being a Jesus consumer. Most people come into faith as consumers, not followers. They hear stories about how sin destroys people's lives. Faith is the antidote to that destruction. It protects them. It makes their lives better. It serves them. So, why not adopt some faith?

But faith is tested when the going gets tough, when it begins to cost us something. At the end of Jesus' earthly ministry when he was arrested in the Garden of Gethsemane, the New Testament tells us that his followers abandoned him. Whether they knew it or not, they were following Jesus because of what was in it for them. And when he was arrested, there didn't seem to be much benefit to following anymore.

They were consumers. When you're a consumer instead of a follower, life's circumstances will eventually rob you of your faith.

DISCUSSION STARTER

Talk about something you really wanted in life, whether during adulthood or when you were a child. What did you do to try to get it? Did you succeed?

VIDEO OVERVIEW
For Session 6 of the DVD

Even though Jesus' disciples behaved like consumers and not followers when he was arrested, that changed after his resurrection. The very men who abandoned him went on to give up their personal agendas in order to embrace God's agenda. They became full-fledged followers of Jesus. They gave their lives not for what Jesus taught but for what they said they saw: a resurrected Savior.

All of them, that is, except one.

Judas Iscariot never surrendered his own agenda. He never made the transition from consumer to follower. The Gospels tell an interesting story about Judas that gives us insight into what it looks like to cling to our own agendas rather than follow Jesus. The story takes place shortly before Jesus' arrest:

While Jesus was in Bethany in the home of Simon the Leper, a woman came to him with an alabaster jar of very expensive perfume, which she poured on his head as he was reclining at the table.

When the disciples saw this, they were indignant. "Why this waste?" they asked. "This perfume could have been sold at a high price and the money given to the poor."
Matthew 26:6–9

Now, John's gospel gives us some additional detail that reveals the disciples didn't just get indignant; Judas stirred them up:

But one of his disciples, Judas Iscariot, who was later to betray him, objected, "Why wasn't this perfume sold and the money given to the poor? It was worth a year's wages." He did not say this because he cared about the poor but because he was a thief; as keeper of the money bag, he used to help himself to what was put into it.
John 12:4–6

Judas had his own agenda. He was a consumer of Jesus. He was in it for the power, influence, and even money he believed he could get once Jesus fulfilled his role as Messiah by overthrowing the Roman government and becoming king. This is what most Jewish people in the first century assumed the Messiah would do. So, John tells us that Judas wasn't really offended because the perfume could have been sold and used to feed the poor instead of being poured over Jesus. He was upset because he was a thief. Not selling the perfume meant there was less money in the purse for him to steal.

Back in Matthew's gospel, we read Jesus' response to the disciples' indignation:

> *Aware of this, Jesus said to them, "Why are you bothering this woman? She has done a beautiful thing to me. The poor you will always have with you, but you will not always have me. When she poured this perfume on my body, she did it to prepare me for burial."*
> **Matthew 26:10–15**

Jesus knows that Judas isn't actually concerned for the poor. He also knows that the disciples can't see what is coming. They don't know that within days Jesus will be arrested, tried, and crucified. They don't know that three days later, God will raise him from the dead. The world, and their lives, will never be the same. Their perspective is all wrong. But his correction didn't soften Judas' heart:

> Then one of the Twelve—the one called Judas Iscariot—went to the chief priests and asked, "What are you willing to give me if I deliver him over to you?" So they counted out for him thirty pieces of silver.
> **Matthew 26:14–15**

For two thousand years, people have tried to figure out why Judas betrayed Jesus. The best educated guess is that he thought he could force Jesus' hand. He thought he could pressure Jesus into proclaiming himself the king of Israel. That didn't work out so well.

It's easy for us to condemn Judas' shortsightedness and selfishness. But think about how we treat God. We act like we can manipulate him, call him into our world, and get him to do what we want him to do. Then we tell him to stay in the corner until we need him again. We try to turn him into a hip-pocket God. We want him along when we have a big presentation at work or we're waiting for a call from the doctor. But we're not taking him on that vacation to Las Vegas. We're not inviting him to that business dinner because we don't want him to know what it's going to take to close the deal. In fact, we don't even think it's any of his business.

Here's a disturbing but good piece of news: *that* God doesn't exist.

VIDEO NOTES

DISCUSSION QUESTIONS

1. Have you ever seen someone put aside his or her wants in order to follow God's will? How did that person's actions influence your own faith?

2. Talk about a time when you felt a tension between God's will and your own. What did you do?

3. In the video, Andy said, *"God's hand can't be forced. His will can't be thwarted. That god doesn't exist."* How does that statement challenge the way you think about God? What comfort do you find in it?

4. In what ways do you find yourself treating God like a "hip-pocket God"?

5. Have you ever had to give something up—a dream, an ambition, money, career advancement—in order to follow Jesus? Explain.

6. What is one area of your life in which you need to say no to yourself and follow Jesus? What can this group do to support you?

MOVING FORWARD

We all begin our relationship with Jesus just like Judas. We have a plan and we hang onto it and think God will help us accomplish it. We want to believe that our will lines up with God's will. But as we follow Jesus, he begins to pry our little fingers away from our agendas. He begins to show us that our will and God's will are sometimes in conflict.

When your agenda competes with God's, Jesus will challenge you to put aside your agenda. In those moments, it will feel like death because the agenda you're giving up is so central to who you think you are. But don't fear. Surrendering your agenda is a defining moment. When you decide to follow Jesus *even* when it means giving up what you want, you'll discover who you really are. More important, you'll discover *whose* you really are.

CHANGING YOUR MIND

"Father, if you are willing, take this cup from me; yet not my will, but yours be done."
Luke 22:42

PREPARATION FOR SESSION 7

To prepare for Session 7, use these devotions during the week leading up to your small group meeting.

DAY ONE

Read Mark 10:32–37. In the passage, James and John seem oblivious to everything Jesus has just told them. In what ways do we hear what we want to hear from Scripture and ignore what doesn't align with our expectations?

DAY TWO

Read Mark 10:35–37. In what ways are you sometimes tempted to try to use God's power and influence for your own gain?

DAY THREE

Read Mark 10:42. What are some examples of times when you've experienced this kind of leadership in your own life?

DAY FOUR

Read Mark 10:42–43. Have you ever followed someone who leveraged his or her influence on your behalf? How effective was that person as a leader?

DAY FIVE

Read Mark 10:42–45. As a leader, what are some practical ways you can grow toward serving others rather than being served?

Session 7

LEADING GREAT

Jesus was an extraordinary *leader*. He didn't come as a religious figure. He came to bring about extraordinary change. Unfortunately, our cultural pictures of Jesus—handed down through art, literature, and movies—aren't particularly leadership oriented.

In paintings, Jesus is often pale and frail. In movies, he has to be helped into boats because he's basically wearing a skirt. He comes across as kind of weak and ineffectual. He might even seem a little nerdy. But there's no way we'd be talking about Jesus two thousand years later if there wasn't something extraordinary about his leadership.

Think of Jesus' leadership this way. In a mere three years he built his brand. Two millennia later, there are thousands of franchises of that brand all over the world. And Jesus didn't rack up a single frequent-flier mile establishing and spreading those franchises. He did it all from a relatively small piece of land in the backwaters of the Roman Empire. *That's* extraordinary.

In this session, we're going to look at a passage of Scripture in which Jesus gives us his secret to great leadership. If you're a follower of Jesus, this is the kind of leadership he has invited and even commanded you to imitate.

DISCUSSION STARTER

What famous leader do you most admire? What do you admire about that person?

VIDEO OVERVIEW
For Session 7 of the DVD

After Jesus established his church and it began to grow, his disciples were in positions of authority. They had spent three years in close contact with Jesus. People new to the faith looked to them for wisdom about what it looked like to follow Jesus.

Before his crucifixion and resurrection, Jesus had a conversation with his disciples about how to lead. The conversation happened as a result of a conflict among the disciples. The story took place shortly before Jesus' arrest, at a time when the religious and political pressure was building on him and his followers. It's found in the gospel of Mark.

> They were on their way up to Jerusalem, with Jesus leading the way, and the disciples were astonished, while those who followed were afraid. Again he took the Twelve aside and told them what was going to happen to him. "We are going up to Jerusalem," he said, "and the Son of Man will be delivered over to the chief priests and the teachers of the law. They will condemn him to death and will hand him over to the Gentiles, who will mock him and spit on him, flog him and kill him. Three days later he will rise."

Then James and John, the sons of Zebedee, came to him.
"Teacher," they said, "we want you to do for us whatever
we ask."

"What do you want me to do for you?" he asked.

They replied, "Let one of us sit at your right and the other
at your left in your glory."
Mark 10:32–37

This is such a strange beginning to the story. Jesus was trying
to prepare his disciples for the terrible events to come, events
that would shake the foundation of their faith. And it's as though
James and John didn't even hear what he was saying. Instead,
they asked if they could sit at his right and left when he finally
powered up and established his kingdom. More than anything,
they wanted to make sure they were as close as possible to the
source of power and influence.

Just as interesting is how the other disciples responded:

When the ten heard about this, they became indignant
with James and John.
Mark 10:41

The other ten disciples weren't indignant because James and

John were insensitive to Jesus. They were indignant because they wanted to be on Jesus' right and left too. Who did James and John think they were to ask if they could be closest to Jesus?

So, now we get to Jesus' big statement about leadership. In the next verses, he not only explains how he has led them over the past three years, but also how he expects them to lead once the church is established and they're in positions of authority.

> Jesus called them together and said, "You know that those who are regarded as rulers of the Gentiles lord it over them, and their high officials exercise authority over them. Not so with you. Instead, whoever wants to become great among you must be your servant, and whoever wants to be first must be slave of all.
> **Mark 10:42–44**

We all know how leadership works in the world around us. People with authority leverage it for their own benefit. If you're the boss, everyone over whom you have authority is there for your pleasure. They must do your bidding. It's all about you because you're on top.

And when you're not on top, it's best to be as close as possible to the person who is on top. That way, you can exert influence. You can make sure the boss's authority works in your favor. That's why James and John asked to be on Jesus' right and left.

But Jesus turned this dynamic on its head. If you want to have authority like Jesus had, you have to be a servant. You have to put the needs of those over whom you have authority ahead of your own. That's how Jesus led.

If you're going to be a Jesus follower—not a consumer but a follower—you have to learn to lead this way. You have to learn to serve the people you lead instead of lording it over them. This isn't intuitive. It's not the way we usually see leadership play out in the world around us. But it's the standard to which Jesus calls his followers.

Great leaders—leaders such as Jesus—leverage their authority for the benefit of the people under their authority. They look around and ask those they lead, "What can I do to help?"

VIDEO NOTES

Matthew 20:20-28

Mark 10:32-34, 35 -- Teacher will you do something for me. 37- Grant us to sit one at right hand + one at left in your glory. To be in authority, you have to lead like I do. To be great it means to be lead like I do. Mark 10-32-44 ~~~~~~~~~~~~~~~~~~~~~~~~~~ on the benefits ~~~~~~. Great leaders have humility. as a Christian - a follower of Jesus, that is how you will do it.
Mark 10:45 ~~~~~~~~~ by ~~~~~~~~~~~ ") ransom) ~~

DISCUSSION QUESTIONS

1. Talk about a leader in your life—a parent, boss, or coach—who has had a big influence over you. What about that leader made him or her special?

2. Have you ever been under the authority of a poor leader? If so, what did it cost you?

3. Great leaders ask the question, *"What can I do to help?"* Do you agree? How does that statement challenge your assumptions about leadership?

4. In what ways do you live for your own name and your own glory? What have you gained from approaching life that way? What has it cost you?

5. Over whom do you have authority at work or at home? In light of Andy's teaching, in what ways can you change your current approach to leading?

6. Think about someone you lead. What is one thing you can you do this week to leverage your authority for that person's benefit? What can this group do to support you?

MOVING FORWARD

If you want to lead like Jesus, you're going to have to confront your ego. We've all grown up in a culture that says it's all about us. Our careers, our names, our brands are all that really matter. But if you're going to follow Jesus, it means looking in the mirror and asking yourself this question:

Am I really worth living my life for?

Is your name great enough to give your life to? No. But don't feel bad. That's true of all of us. Unless you're the President of the United States or a famous historical figure, no one but your family will remember you five years after you're gone. If you are a famous historical figure, your memory will go on a little bit longer, but not much in the grand scheme of things.

You have an opportunity and a responsibility to leverage whatever authority God gives you in this life to bring praise and glory to his name. Your name isn't worth living for. Your glory isn't worth living for. God's is.

CHANGING YOUR MIND

"For even the Son of Man did not come to be served, but to serve, and to give his life as a ransom for many."
Mark 10:45

PREPARATION FOR SESSION 8

To prepare for Session 8, use these devotions during the week leading up to your small group meeting.

DAY ONE

Read John 6:48–51. In what ways is Jesus "the bread of life" for you? How do you depend on him each day? What are some ways you need to depend on him more?

DAY TWO

Read John 6:53–55. Jesus' audience found his words shocking and upsetting. In what ways is the idea of dependence on God shocking and upsetting to people living today?

DAY THREE

Read John 6:60–61. What are some of Jesus' teachings that you find "hard"? What are some practical things you do to follow Jesus faithfully and without grumbling when what he asks is challenging?

DAY FOUR

Read John 6:65–66. As you think about the passage, consider the things that caused some of Jesus' disciples to quit following him. Do the temptations they faced sound real and compelling to you? Why or why not?

DAY FIVE

Read John 6:67–69. Consider Simon Peter's response in this passage. How does it reflect your own response when following Jesus becomes difficult?

Session 8

UNFOLLOW

Everyone is invited to follow Jesus. It doesn't matter what you've done or haven't done. It doesn't matter who you know or don't know. It doesn't matter how much you've been to church or haven't been to church. Jesus offers an open invitation to everyone.

Jesus invites you to relationship, not church or religion. His invitation isn't about what you should or shouldn't do. It's an invitation to a personal relationship with an invisible God who revealed himself through his Son, who was a visible person: the Lord Jesus Christ.

Being a sinner doesn't disqualify you from Jesus' invitation. In fact, it's a prerequisite to being invited. Everyone who followed Jesus in the first century and everyone who has followed him since was a sinner.

Doubt doesn't disqualify you from Jesus' invitation. It's a prerequisite to being invited. Even Jesus' first-century followers—the ones who ate with him and camped with him, had face-to-face conversations with him, and witnessed him performing miracles—doubted right up to the end. Their doubts were only swept away when they saw him resurrected and were able to touch the nail wounds in his hands.

Jesus urges you to bring your sin and your doubt and follow him. He wants to lead you to a faith that overwhelms fear. Why should you be afraid when the God who created the universe knows you and cares about you? We can face crisis and trouble fearlessly with a confidence in God that allows us to overcome our circumstances.

That's where Jesus leads ... if you'll just follow.

In this final session we're going to talk about an extraordinarily important question. It's important because somewhere along the way in every single person's faith journey is a temptation to hit the "Unfollow" button. If you haven't faced this temptation yet, you will. And when you do, you need to ask this question before you unfollow Jesus.

DISCUSSION STARTER

What is the most valuable thing you learned during this study? What is the most challenging principle to apply?

VIDEO OVERVIEW
For Session 8 of the DVD

John's gospel records an event in which Jesus miraculously fed five thousand people with five small barley loaves and two small fish. Afterward, the crowd was so amazed that they wanted to immediately crown Jesus king. But Jesus got into a boat and crossed the Sea of Galilee to a town called Capernaum. He began to teach in Capernaum, but some of the people who had witnessed the feeding of the five thousand showed up and started stirring up the crowd. They wanted to see Jesus perform another miracle.

Jesus decided to use this moment as a creative teaching opportunity. He explained that he fed them bread and fish, and now they're hungry again because that's how our bodies work. A meal doesn't satisfy us forever. But God can provide food for our souls that fills us up forever. And then Jesus said this:

> Jesus said to them, "Very truly I tell you, unless you eat the flesh of the Son of Man and drink his blood, you have no life in you. Whoever eats my flesh and drinks my blood has eternal life, and I will raise them up at the last day."
> **John 6:53–54**

It should come as no surprise that this had the effect of thinning the crowd. What Jesus said sounded like cannibalism. It sounded sacrilegious. It certainly wasn't something they wanted their children to hear.

> *On hearing it, many of his disciples said, "This is a hard teaching. Who can accept it?"*

> *Aware that his disciples were grumbling about this, Jesus said to them, "Does this offend you?"*

> *From this time many of his disciples turned back and no longer followed him.*
> **John 6:60–61, 66**

"Disciples" here doesn't refer to the Twelve but to the larger crowds that had been following Jesus around the countryside, listening to his teachings and seeing him perform miracles. Suddenly, they weren't on board anymore. They were beginning to hit the Unfollow button. They loved the miracles. They loved the healing. They loved the excitement. They loved the thought that Jesus might proclaim himself king and overthrow their Roman occupiers. But the stuff about eating his flesh and drinking his blood was too much.

Jesus knew the hearts of people, so he paused in his sermon, turned to the Twelve, and asked them if they were going to leave him too. Were they going to press the Unfollow button?

This is a relevant question for us too. Regardless of how long we've followed Jesus, the day will come when we're tempted to unfollow. You may think it'll never happen to you, but it will. It usually comes during a time of transition, temptation, or trouble. It may be when a job moves you from a familiar city to one that's unfamiliar. Transition shakes up your life. You're tempted to press Unfollow. It may be that your faith begins to get in the way of a romantic relationship or makes you feel guilty about your weekend fun. Suddenly, Jesus is in the way. He's inconvenient. And you're tempted to press Unfollow. Or it may be that you face financial challenges and following Jesus isn't helping. In fact, at least in the short term, it's making things worse. You're tempted to press Unfollow.

But in that dramatic moment when Jesus asked the Twelve if they were going to leave him too, Peter said something brilliant. That's a big deal because most of the time in these situations, Peter said the wrong thing. But this time he asked a question that cut to the heart of their dilemma, and it cuts to heart of our dilemmas when our faith is shaken. It's this:

> Simon Peter answered him, "Lord, to whom shall we go? You have the words of eternal life. We have come to believe and to know that you are the Holy One of God."
> **John 6:68–69**

No one else offers what Jesus offers. Peter could remember when he was on a fishing boat with his father, and Jesus came along and asked Peter to follow him into a life of greater purpose. Peter was invited into the story of God. He was invited into history. If he left Jesus, where was he going to go? Would he go back to being a fisherman? Would he go back to a small life, disconnected from God grand story? In that moment, regardless of the thinning crowds and the weird things Jesus had just said, Peter remembered that he'd been given the opportunity to follow the Savior of the world. How could he turn back?

Transition + temptations always create questions.
Don't make a move until you can answer the question - To whom shall I go?

VIDEO NOTES

everyone is invited to follow Jesus
Being a sinner is a prerequisite
Its an invitation to relationship
Having doubts is a prerequisite

Goal is overwhelming faith
Followers dress alike CHK FLK PG
Following eventually cost you something
but not following may cost you everything.
Followers are great leaders

Regular Bread will fill you temporarily
God will fill you up forever
He began to compare himself to
bread as "bread of life"

People become an unfollower when it becomes
too hard to follow.

When you choose not to follow Jesus
you will be following something or
someone. So if you don't follow
Jesus, then whom? Live for something
rather than live for nothing. What does 101
anyone else have to offers. - Probably
empty promises.

DISCUSSION QUESTIONS

1. Talk about a time when you were embarrassed by a friend or family member. How did you respond?

2. Read John 6:56–61. Are there things Jesus said or did that offend you or that used to offend you? Explain.

3. In the video, Andy said, *"Questions are important because considering options always brings clarity."* Do you agree? Why or why not?

4. Talk about a major transition in your life. How did that event affect your faith?

5. When has following Jesus been inconvenient, embarrassing, or costly for you? What did you do?

6. Is transition, trouble, or temptation currently getting in the way of your ability to follow Jesus? What can this group do to support you?

MOVING FORWARD

Transition, temptation, and trouble always create questions.

Where's God? Why would God allow this to happen? Why didn't God come through for me?

It's okay to ask those questions. God is big enough to handle them. But it's a mistake to step away from Jesus just because you have questions and the answers aren't immediately apparent. After you've considered all of the questions and sorted through all the options, ask yourself another question. Ask the question that Peter asked:

To whom shall I go?

Salvation is free. Following Jesus will cost you something. But refusing to follow Jesus could cost you *everything*.

CHANGING YOUR MIND

"We have come to believe and to know that you are the Holy One of God."
John 6:69

Leader's Guide

LEADING THE DISCUSSION

You probably have a mental picture of what it will look like to lead—what you'll say and how group members will respond. Before you get too far into planning, there are some things you should know about leading a small group discussion.

CULTIVATE DISCUSSION.

It's easy to assume that a group meeting lives or dies on the quality of your ideas. That's not true. It's the ideas of everyone in the group that make a small group meeting successful. Your role is to create an environment in which people feel safe to share their thoughts. That's how relationships will grow and thrive among your group members.

Here's a basic truth about spiritual growth within the context of community: the study materials aren't as important as the relationships through which those materials take practical shape in the lives of the group members. The more meaningful the relationships, the more meaningful the study. The best materials in the world won't change lives in a sterile environment.

POINT TO THE MATERIAL.

A good host or hostess creates an environment where people

can connect relationally. He or she knows when to help guests connect and when to stay out of the way when those connections are happening organically. As a small group leader, sometimes you'll simply read a discussion question and invite everyone to respond. The conversation will take care of itself. At other times, you may need to encourage group members to share their ideas. Remember, some of the best insights will come from the people in your group. Go with the flow, but be ready to nudge the conversation in the right direction when necessary.

DEPART FROM THE MATERIAL.

We've carefully designed this study for your small group. We've written the materials and designed the questions to elicit the kinds of conversations we think will be most helpful to your group members. That doesn't mean you should stick rigidly to the materials. Knowing when to depart from them is more art than science, but no one knows more about your group than you do.

The stories, questions, and exercises are here to provide a framework for exploration. But different groups have different chemistries and different motivations. Sometimes the best way to start a small group discussion is to ask, "Does anyone have a personal insight you'd like to share from this week's material?" Then sit back and listen.

STAY ON TRACK.

This is the flip side to the previous point. There's an art to facilitating an engaging conversation. While you want to leave space for group members to think through the discussion, you also need to keep your objectives in mind. Make sure the discussion is contributing to the bottom line for the week. Don't let the discussion veer off into tangents. Interject politely in order to refocus the group.

PRAY.

This is the most important thing you can do as a leader. The best leaders get out of God's way and let him communicate through them. Remember: books don't teach God's Word; neither do sermons or discussion groups. God speaks into the hearts of men and women. Prayer is a vital part of communicating with him.

Pray for your group members. Pray for your own leadership. Pray that God is not only present at your group meetings but is directing them.

SESSION 1: NOTES FOR LEADING

BIG IDEA: Jesus invites unbelievers and misbehavers to follow him.

TO PREPARE TO LEAD THE FIRST SESSION:

- Read Matthew 9:9–13.

- Pray that you and your group members begin the study with hearts and minds open to what God wants to show you.

DISCUSSION STARTER

The Discussion Starter is designed to act as an icebreaker. Some of the questions may feel a little random, but they're intended to help your group members warm up by talking about a common experience or tension. They're usually related in some way to the session's topic but are intended to get your group members talking about their personal experiences without delving into theology or doctrine.

The Session 1 Discussion Starter is meant to get you thinking about examples of leadership in your own life and what makes a leader worth following.

DISCUSSION QUESTIONS

1. **Did you grow up in a church that emphasized doing what Jesus says over following him? Or if you didn't grow up going to church, did you assume that's what Christianity was all about? How has the "Jesus says" mindset affected your spiritual journey so far?**

2. **Jesus was extraordinarily comfortable with people who**

were nothing like him. How might your community, your nation, and the world be different if the church treated people the way Jesus did?

The first two questions are a great opportunity for you to begin to take the pulse of your group members as it relates to their experiences in church (good and bad), and whether they carry with them a spiritual history of following rules as opposed to following Jesus.

3. In Jesus' culture, tax collectors were considered the lowest of the low. What kinds of people occupy that position in our culture? Is it challenging for you to believe that Jesus would extend an offer to those people to follow him? Why or why not?

4. How comforting is the idea that Jesus wants everyone to follow him regardless of what they believe or how they behave? How is it challenging?

The next two questions challenge you and your group members to begin to assess how religion may stand between you and people who are different from you. Try to help your group members push past giving the "right" answers and to be open and transparent about how they struggle to accept others (we all struggle with this). Ask clarifying questions to get the conversation flowing. Being open and transparent yourself will give group members permission to speak freely.

5. What are some things that make it difficult for you to follow Jesus?

6. What is one thing you can do this week to begin to follow Jesus or to follow him more closely? What can this group do to support you?

The last two questions delve into the area of personal application. *Knowing* doesn't cause us to grow. *Doing* causes us to grow. If group members can think of and follow through on a personal action step that is simple, achievable, and measurable, they will be more likely grow as a result of the discussion.

SESSION 2: NOTES FOR LEADING

BIG IDEA: Whatever your next step is, take it.

TO PREPARE TO LEAD SESSION 2:

- Read Luke 5:1–11.
- Pray that you and your group members discover the next steps in your spiritual journeys and find the courage and determination to take them.

DISCUSSION STARTER

This question is designed to break the ice by getting you and your group members thinking about the ways you set and pursue real-world goals.

DISCUSSION QUESTIONS

1. Have you ever met a Christian whose faith impressed and intimidated you? How did that person influence your view of Christianity? How did he or she influence your view of your own faith?

This is an entry level question to encourage you and your group members to think of people in your lives who have the kind of faith to which you aspire.

2. Andy challenged you to answer the question, "Am I following Jesus?" As you thought about that question, where did it lead you?
3. What risks do you associate with following Jesus? How do those risks cause you to hesitate?
4. Do you agree with the idea that Christianity isn't a blind faith but an informed faith? Why or why not?

These questions are self-diagnostic. They let you and your group members assess where you are in your spiritual journeys and identify potential obstacles to your growth. In the case of question 4, try to make sure your group members know that it's okay to express disagreement with the message, if that's how they feel. Some of the richest conversations happen when people challenge the material.

5. In the video, Andy talked about four stages of following Jesus—listening and learning; taking a small, inconvenient step; allowing Jesus to do something unusual in one area of your life; and surrendering all aspects of your life to him. Which stage best describes where you are right now? Explain.

Since this session is about figuring out your next step and then taking it, it's important for you and your group members to know where you are now in order to know where you need to go next.

6. Based on where you are right now, what is your next step in following Jesus? What can this group do to support you?

Think this question through in advance. Having a concrete next step yourself will help your group members define next steps for themselves.

SESSION 3: NOTES FOR LEADING

BIG IDEA: The opposite of faith is fear. The end game of following Jesus is fearless faith—faith that overwhelms fear. What would you do if you were confident God was with you? That's how Jesus lived. That's how those who follow Jesus live.

TO PREPARE FOR THIS SESSION:

- Read Matthew 10.

- Pray that God walks with you and your group members and shows you how to develop faith that overwhelms fear.

DISCUSSION STARTER

Talking about our strange superstitions is a light conversation starter. But our superstitions are also usually linked to the things we fear. You don't need to start talking about fear here, but the discussion of superstitions will loosen things up and prepare your group for a deeper discussion.

DISCUSSION QUESTIONS

1. Do you tend to be a worrier or do you deal with circumstances as they come? How is that natural wiring a strength for you? How is it a weakness?

2. What circumstances, consequences, or possibilities do you fear? How does that fear limit your choices in life?

The first two questions challenge you and your group members to talk with increasing depth about your personal fears.

3. Think about a time when you felt close to God. Were your circumstances at that time good or bad? How did those circumstances, good or bad, influence your relationship with God?

Some of your group members may have felt closest to God when their circumstances were good, but many will have felt closest to him when times were tough. It's good to remind ourselves that life's challenges can benefit us if they draw us closer to our heavenly Father.

4. **Have you ever met someone who was choosing to trust God through difficult circumstances? Can you imagine yourself having a faith like that? Why or why not?**

This questions gives you and your group members the opportunity to tell inspiring stories and to imagine how your faith might grow through difficult circumstances.

5. **What hopes or dreams might you miss out on if you were to let fear control your life?**

6. **What circumstances do you face right now that you need to entrust to God? What worries are you struggling with that you need to entrust to God? What can this group do to support you?**

As in previous weeks, use these questions to help your group members personalize and apply the session's big idea. One of the best ways to do that is to personalize and apply it yourself.

SESSION 4: NOTES FOR LEADING

BIG IDEA: Jesus followers should be recognizable by what they wear.

TO PREPARE TO LEAD THIS SESSION:

- Read Colossians 3:1–17. During your group discussion, you'll focus on verses 12 and 13, but studying the longer passage will give you additional context to help you lead well.
- Pray that God grows you and your group members in your ability to live in a way that reflects Christ's love.

DISCUSSION STARTER

This session's discussion starter is a light icebreaker to help you and your group members open up and have some fun.

DISCUSSION QUESTIONS

1. When you think of the word "Christian," what qualities come to mind? Are they positive or negative? Why?
2. Talk about a time when you encountered a Christian who was more interested in making a point than making a difference. How did that person affect the way you view Jesus?

The first two questions allow your group members to process and discuss how their own view of faith and even of God has been shaped by other people's prioritizing religion over relationship .

3. In the video, Andy said, *"All religions gravitate toward rule keeping instead of relationship building."* Do you agree with that statement? Why or why not?

Ask clarifying questions and encourage your group members so they know that if they disagree with any part of Andy's teaching, it's okay for them to say so.

4. As you think about compassion, kindness, humility, and gentleness, which seems like it would be most difficult to live out in your relationships with others? Why?

5. Read Colossians 3:12–14. What are some of the challenges to living the kind of life Jesus calls his followers to live?

6. Think of one person in your life who is difficult to love. What is one thing you can do this week to better love that person? What can this group do to support you?

As you move through questions 4 through 6, help your group members begin to apply the session's big idea in practical ways.

SESSION 5: NOTES FOR LEADING

BIG IDEA: Deny yourself now or lose yourself later. Following Jesus will eventually cost you something.

TO PREPARE TO LEAD THIS SESSION:

- Read Mark 8:27–38.

- Pray that you and your group members stand firm when difficult circumstances challenge your faith.

DISCUSSION STARTER

Remember that the Discussion Starter is an icebreaker. Try to keep the conversation light. But this question is designed to touch on your aspirations. For some, that can be a tough conversation.

DISCUSSION QUESTIONS

1. **Talk about a time when you knew you were supposed to do something that was difficult. Did you do it? What was the outcome?**

This is a chance for you to make the connection that there's usually a long-term payoff to doing something that's difficult in the short term.

2. **Talk about a time when you've seen someone demonstrate extraordinary faith in the midst of difficult circumstances. How did that change or influence your view of faith?**

Question 2 is similar to Question 4 in Session 3, but this time instead of you and your group members imagining living with big faith, you'll talk about how another person's faith during tough times actually influenced your own faith.

3. **Have you ever seen someone else pay a price for his or her decision to follow Jesus? How did that person's experiences influence your own faith?**

This is an opportunity for you and your group members to talk about hardship and adversity without delving into personal examples.

4. **Has your faith ever cost you something? If so, how has paying that cost changed your relationship with God?**

Now begin to personalize the previous question.

5. **Read Mark 8:34–36. How do Jesus' words challenge you? In what ways do they give you comfort?**
6. **Are you currently being nudged to do something, say something, quit something, start something, or give up something? What can this group do to support you?**

This can potentially be an easy application to skip. Encourage your group members to really think about how God is currently working in their lives, and talk about any changes they feel prompted to make in their lives.

SESSION 6: NOTES FOR LEADING

BIG IDEA: It's better to follow God's will than attempt to impose our own. God's hand can't be forced. His will can't be thwarted.

TO PREPARE TO LEAD THIS SESSION:

- Read John 12:1–11 and Matthew 26:6–16.
- Pray that God helps you and your group members to learn more and more how to submit to his will in your lives.

DISCUSSION STARTER

This question is about the lengths we'll go to satisfy our own desires. That can be a deep topic, but small examples are fine. Try to keep things light. This is an icebreaker.

DISCUSSION QUESTIONS

1. **Have you ever seen someone put aside his or her wants in order to follow God's will? How did that person's actions influence your own faith?**

This is an opportunity for you and your group members to explore how your faith has been influenced by the examples of others.

2. **Talk about a time when you felt a tension between God's will and your own. What did you do?**

3. In the video, Andy said, *"God's hand can't be forced. His will can't be thwarted. That god doesn't exist."* How does that statement challenge the way you think about God? What comfort do you find in it?

4. In what ways do you find yourself treating God like a "hip-pocket God"?

In questions 2, 3, and 4, you and your group members will talk at varying depths about how you've experienced a tension between God's will and your desires.

5. Have you ever had to give something up—a dream, an ambition, money, career advancement—in order to follow Jesus? Explain.

Your group can now personalize what you discussed in Question 1.

6. What is one area of your life in which you need to say no to yourself and follow Jesus? What can this group do to support you?

Each of us has areas of our lives in which we need to submit to God. It's important to our growth that we name them and begin to take steps to submit.

SESSION 7: NOTES FOR LEADING

BIG IDEA: Leverage your authority for the benefit of those under your authority.

TO PREPARE TO LEAD THIS SESSION:

- Read Mark 10:32–44.
- Pray that you and your group members continue to develop humility and servants' hearts as you grow in your relationship with Jesus.

DISCUSSION STARTER

This is a light question that will also allow you and your group members to start to think about what makes a great leader great.

DISCUSSION QUESTIONS

1. **Talk about a leader in your life—a parent, boss, or coach— who has had a big influence over you. What about that leader made him or her special?**

This question is similar to the Discussion Starter, but it takes things out of the realm of famous leaders and into the realm of those who have personally influenced your lives.

2. **Have you ever been under the authority of a poor leader? If so, what did it cost you?**

Keep in mind that you're exploring, directly or indirectly, the qualities that make great leaders.

3. Great leaders ask the question, *"What can I do to help?"* Do you agree? How does that statement challenge your assumptions about leadership?

Allow room for your group members to disagree with the message. It's okay if they dissent. In fact, it can improve the quality and helpfulness of the group discussion.

4. In what ways do you live for your own name and your own glory? What have you gained from approaching life that way? What has it cost you?

5. Over whom do you have authority at work or at home? In light of Andy's teaching, in what ways can you change your current approach to leading?

6. Think about someone you lead. What is one thing you can you do this week to leverage your authority for that person's benefit? What can this group do to support you?

The final three questions lead toward personal application. For some people, it's obvious in which realms of life they lead as well as whom they lead. Others may have to think about where they've been given leadership responsibilities. Either way, nearly every adult plays the role of a leader in some area of life.

SESSION 8: NOTES FOR LEADING

BIG IDEA: If you don't follow Jesus, to whom will you turn?

TO PREPARE TO LEAD THIS FINAL SESSION:

- Read John 6:25–71.

- Thank your heavenly Father for what you've learned over the course of this study and for how you and your group members have grown closer. Pray that God helps you to continue to apply what you've learned and to grow closer to him.

DISCUSSION STARTER

This question is an opportunity for you to review what you've experienced together during this study. If you've seen life-change in the members of your group, make sure you take time to point it out and celebrate it.

DISCUSSION QUESTIONS

1. **Talk about a time when you were embarrassed by a friend or family member. How did you respond?**

This question is an icebreaker, but it will help your group members to gauge their natural response to embarrassment.

2. **Read John 6:56–61. Are there things Jesus said or did that offend you or that used to offend you? Explain.**

3. In the video, Andy said, *"Questions are important because considering options always brings clarity."* Do you agree? Why or why not?

As always, provide space for group members to say surprising (but honest) things and to disagree with the message. Make sure they feel safe doing so.

4. Talk about a major transition in your life. How did that event affect your faith?

5. When has following Jesus been inconvenient, embarrassing, or costly for you? What did you do?

6. Is transition, trouble, or temptation currently getting in the way of your ability to follow Jesus? What can this group do to support you?

Use Questions 4 through 6 to personalize and apply the big idea.

End the group session in prayer. Ask your group members if there are things that came up during the course of the study about which they would like the group to provide continued encouragement or accountability.

Christian DVD Study
It's Not What You Think

Andy Stanley

According to Andy Stanley, the words used to describe Christians today often bear no resemblance to what Jesus wanted his followers to be known for.

In this eight-session video study (participant's guide sold separately), you'll learn:

- What one word should be descriptive of every Christian
- How Jesus' followers should treat those who are outside the faith
- Why people love Jesus but can't stand his followers

What does is mean to be Christian? Curiously, the term is never used in Scripture. Instead, Christian was a label used by outsiders to define Jesus' followers. Jesus referenced "disciple" as the key word he used to describe his supporters along with the fact that they would be known for their love—a novel concept for their time—and ours today.

Sessions include:

1. Brand Recognition
2. Quitters
3. Insiders, Outsiders
4. Showing Up
5. When Gracie Met Truthy
6. Angry Birds
7. Loopholes
8. Working It Out

Available in stores and online!

How to Be Rich: A DVD Study

It's Not What You Have.
It's What You Do With
What You Have.

Andy Stanley

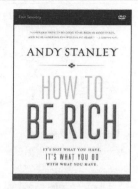

Ever stood in front of a closet full of clothes trying to find something to wear?
Ever traded in a perfectly good car for another...car?
Ever killed some time talking on your cell phone while standing in line to get a newer version of the same phone?

According to author and pastor Andy Stanley, if you answered "yes" to any of those questions, you might be rich.

But you might think, rich is the other guy. Rich is that other family. Rich is having more than you currently have. If that's the case, you can be rich and not know it. You can be rich and not feel it. You can be rich and not act like it. And that is a problem.

In this four-session small group study, Andy Stanley encourages us to consider that we may be richer than we think, and challenges us to consider that we may not be very good at it.

It's one thing to Be Rich.

Andy wants to help us all be GOOD at it!

Sessions include:

1. Congratulations
2. Side Effects
3. Dollar Cost Living
4. Diversify

Guardrails DVD Study

Avoiding Regrets in Your Life

Andy Stanley

[Guardrails: a system designed to keep vehicles from straying into dangerous or off-limit areas.]

They're everywhere, but they don't really get much attention . . . until somebody hits one. And then, more often than not, it is a lifesaver.

Ever wonder what it would be like to have guardrails in other areas of your life—areas where culture baits you to the edge of disaster and then chastises you when you step across the line?

Your friendships. Your finances. Your marriage. Maybe your greatest regret could have been avoided if you had established guardrails.

In this six-session video based study (participant's guide sold separately), Andy Stanley challenges us to stop flirting with disaster and establish some personal guardrails.

Session titles:

1. Direct and Protect
2. Why Can't We Be Friends
3. Flee Baby Flee!
4. Me and the Mrs.
5. The Consumption Assumption
6. Once and For All